Muddy Hands, Sudsy Hands

By Christine Prill
Illustrated by John Konecny

Published by Orange Hat Publishing 2015, 2020
ISBN 978-1-943331-03-1
Second Edition

For information, please contact:

Orange Hat Publishing
www.orangehatpublishing.com
Waukesha, WI

This book is dedicated to my loving family
Marcie, Scott, Emily & Jeff
For all their help and collaboration

And to all adventurous kids in the world whose parents
& families keep them healthy.

A special thanks to Paul S. & Kristina S. for their advice
and assistance in the book publishing process.

Wash your hands

Mom said so

This book belongs to:

_____

Each day
my parents
tell me,
before I eat
each meal,

I love to play outside all day. My fun, it never ends!

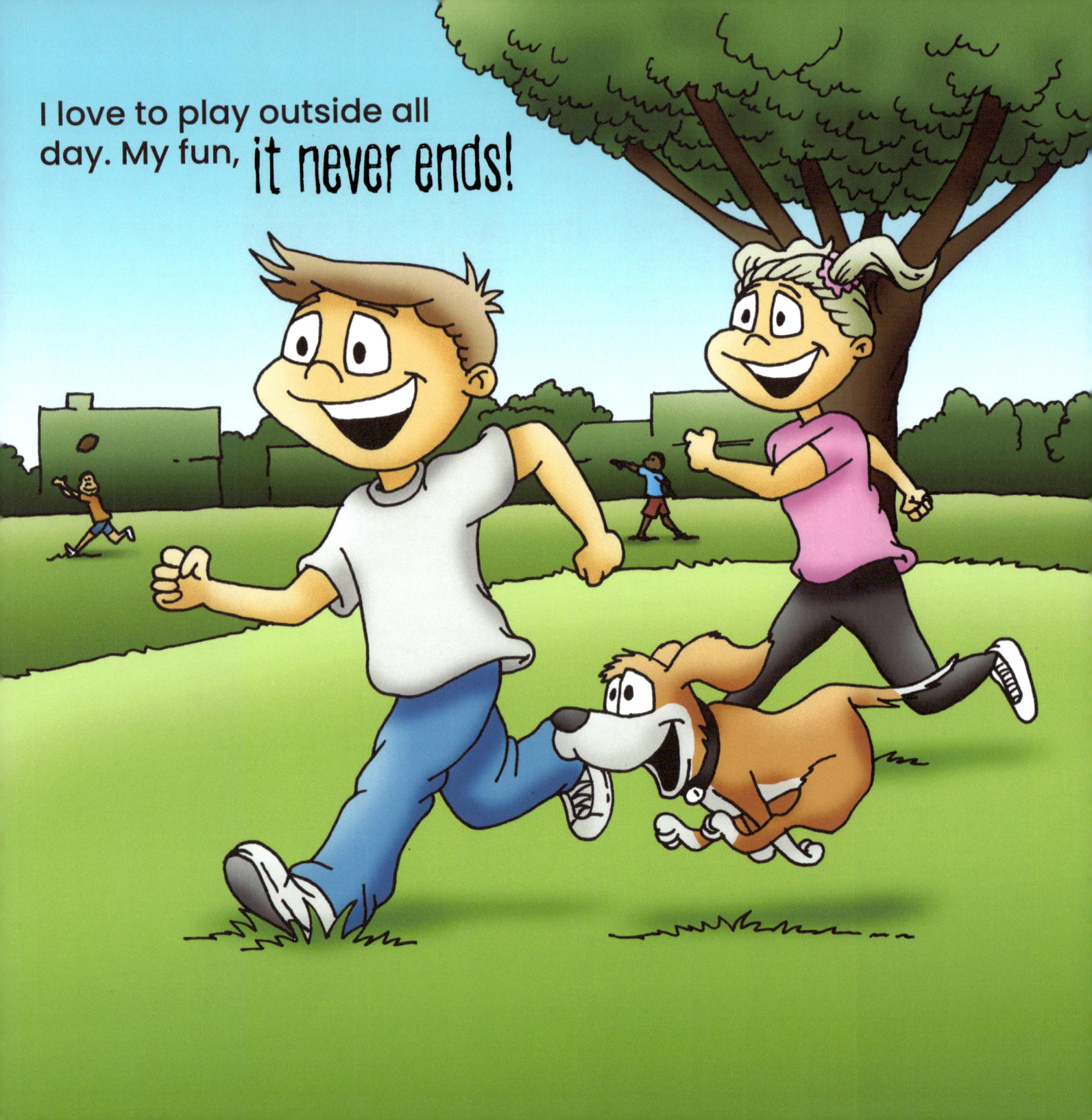

One day I am a **secret spy,**
the next I'm chasing friends.

But I guess I see the point, when looking at my hands.

There's mud **all over** front and back, and look, there's even **sand!**

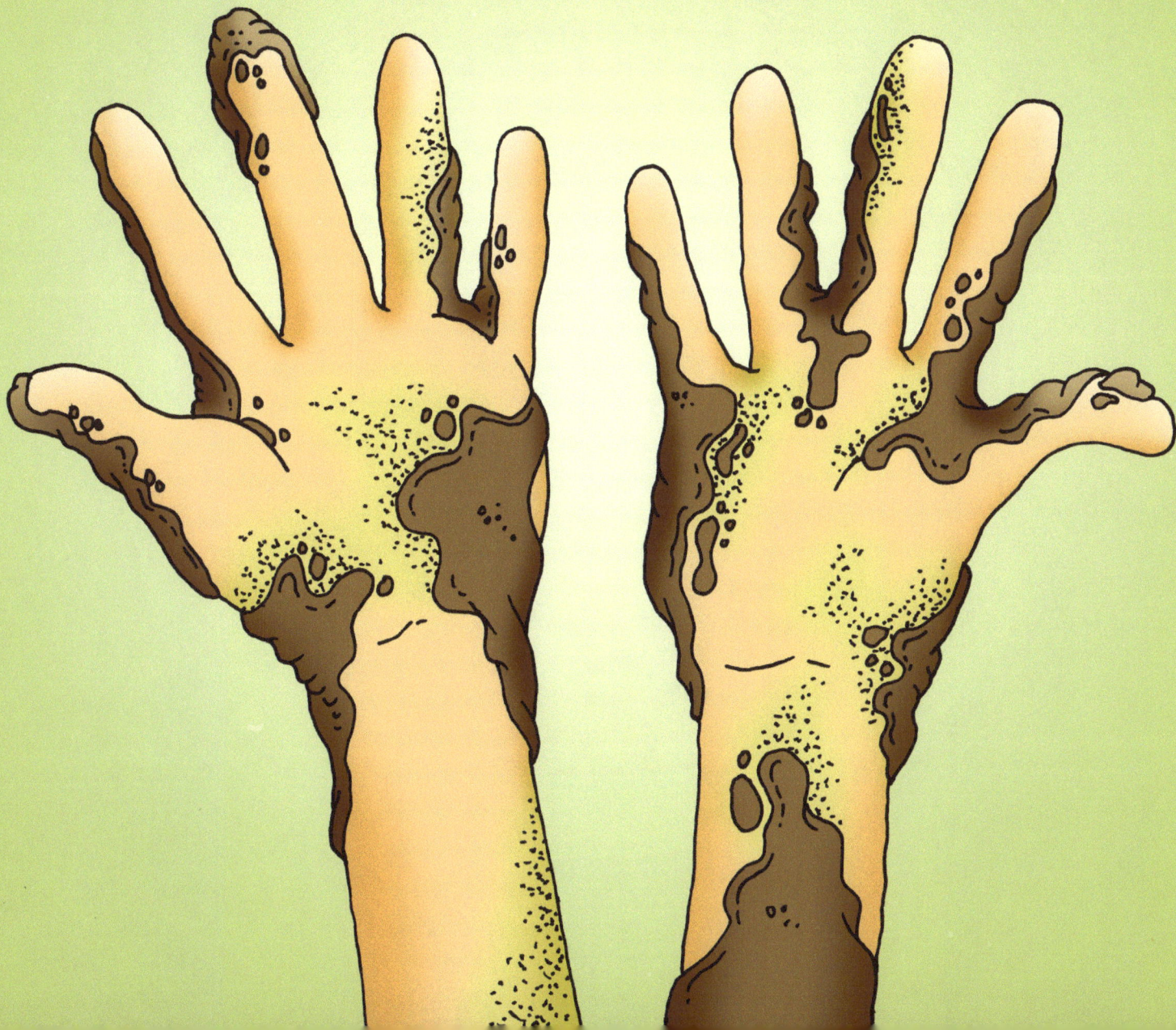

Dirt crunchies on my breakfast, and germs that I can't see—

Who would want that
mud-filled meal?

I don't,
no thanks,
not me!

So when it's
time to pause
my games,
I know what
must be done.

Before I go
and eat
my meal,

it's
time
for
bathroom
fun!

I can turn the faucet on,
for water nice and warm,

A stream of water
and some soap,

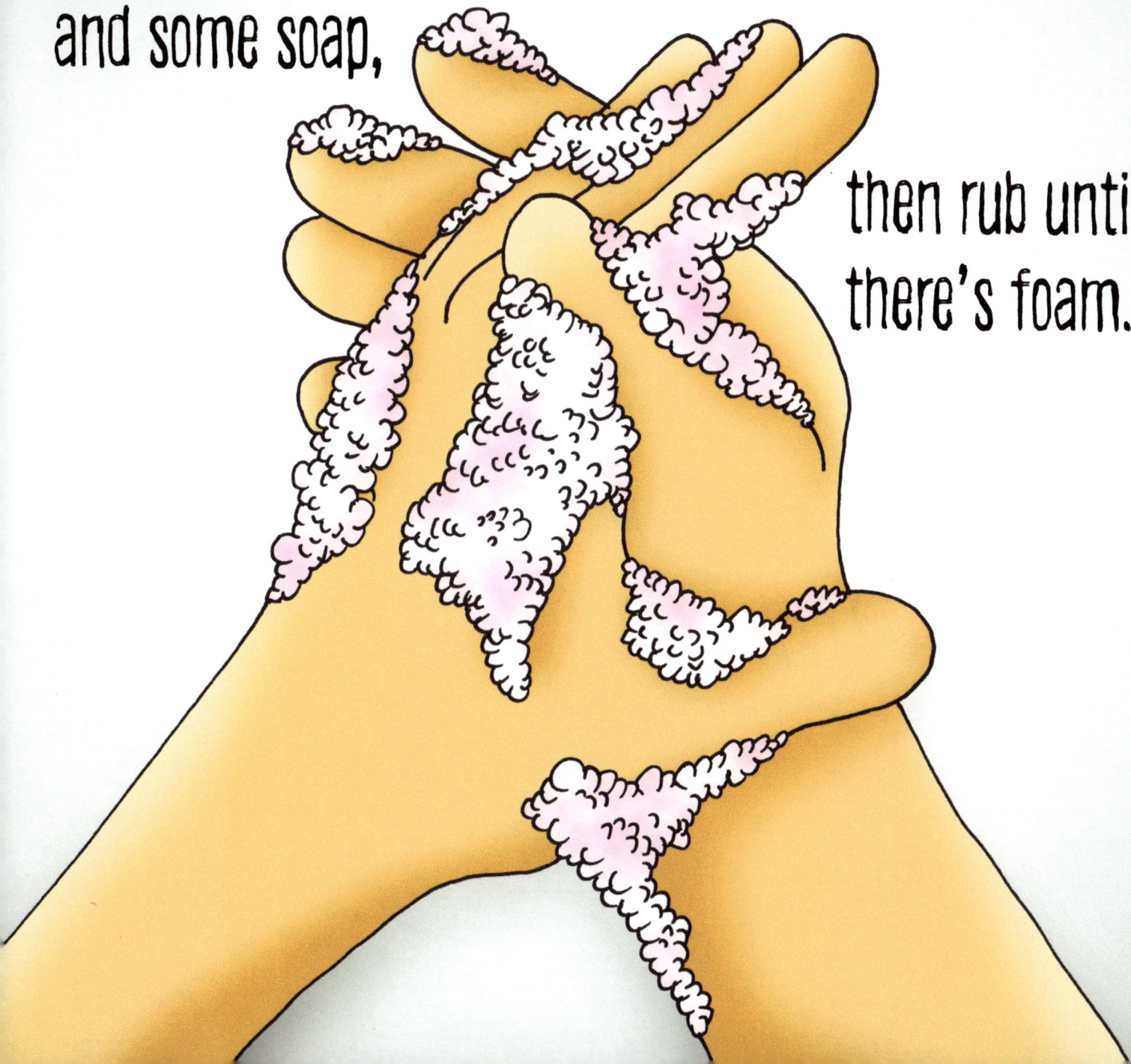

then rub until
there's foam.

Together it all mixes . . .

The suds are all washed free.

"Count to twenty," Mother says, "for hands clean as can be."

All the sap and leaves are gone now. It's perfect timing too—

My tummy growls, I'm hungry. My hands are clean!

YAHOO!

I show my parents my clean hands, and slide into the chair.